SNAPPY INTERVIEWS

100 QUESTIONS
FOR THE ORACLE DBA

Also by Christopher Lawson

The Art & Science of Oracle Performance Tuning

SNAPPY INTERVIEWS
100 QUESTIONS
FOR THE ORACLE DBA

Christopher Lawson

author of
"The Art & Science of
Oracle Performance Tuning"

Snappy Books
San Francisco

Printed in the United States of America.

Snappy Interviews: 100 Questions to Ask Oracle DBAs
Christopher Lawson – 1st ed.

ISBN-10: 1-4348-2620-1
ISBN-13: 9-781-4348-2620-6

Snappy Interviews is a trademark of Snappy Books, San Francisco
Series Editor Christopher Lawson

www.oraclemagician.com

Printed in the United States of America
First Edition
10 9 8 7 6 5 4 3 2 1

ACKNOWLEDGEMENTS

Thanks to the following DBAs for their suggestions: Brian Hanafee, Alex Wong, Bhanu Gandikota, Iggy Fernandez, Danny Chow, Ross Woody, Vasubabu Kavuri, Savita Shukla, Arul Ramachandran, Jeremiah Wilton, Antony Fewster, Brian Hanson, Roger Ruckert, Camilo Tan, Guy Harrison, Sten Rognes, and Thomas Briggs.

The reviewer comments were all very helpful and much appreciated! Of course, the responsibility for any errors is my own.

Finally, special thanks to my first "guinea pig" interview candidate, Hamid Minoui, who helped check the accuracy and fairness of the questions.

CONTENTS

INTRODUCTION

Consider the following actual scenario:

A nervous DBA candidate, kept waiting for 30 minutes, is escorted into the interview room. Instead of setting the candidate at ease, the interviewer begins the interview by displaying the *init.ora* parameter file for one of their databases. He then asks the candidate to explain the meaning of several arcane "underscore" parameters specific to their installation.

Needless to say, the candidate in the above interview above got off to a poor start. In fact, he immediately questioned the fairness of the interview, with thoughts such as, Why are they asking such arcane questions? Are they deliberately trying to fail me?

It should be obvious how unfair and inaccurate are interviewing tactics such as these. Performing a fair interview is a real art. The objective should be to ascertain as accurately and fairly as possible the skill level of the candidate. We're not interested in tricking the candidate, or showing them how deficient their experience is. Instead, we should arrange a scenario that brings out the *best* in the candidate.

SECRET "NICHE" QUESTIONS

I recently reviewed a set of DBA questions that purported to be general interview questions. To my dismay, I perceived that many of the questions were actually "niche" questions that most good DBAs—even those with excellent experience—would not be able to answer. I further detected a slant weighted toward certain types of applications (in this case *Windows*). It seemed to me that the writer was really interviewing for a *clone*, not a DBA with a well-rounded experience.

Almost everyone will agree that questions should fairly measure the skills of the interviewee. What makes this simple objective so challenging, however, is the tendency to inject *bias* into the questions. That is, we all tend to ask questions that reflect our own experience. We take our own experience and *generalize* it, assuming that one person's experience should be applicable to everyone. In doing so, we unwittingly create unfair questions that depend on a narrow (and unrealistic) experience set.

GROUND RULES

The questions in this guide have been selected using this framework:

- Questions should reflect understanding of concepts.
- Questions should reflect actual hands-on experience.
- Questions should *not* be based on memorization of arcane names or syntax.
- Questions should reflect issues seen by the majority of DBAs of that skill level.

The questions in this guide are for determining general DBA skills, not proficiency in a niche skill set. The questions are therefore by necessity general in nature. We don't include questions on RAC, Oracle Financials, Streams, etc., since most DBAs would not be expected to have this type of experience.

FAIR QUESTIONS

The intent of the questions is that *most* DBAs, for a given skill level, can successfully answer *most* of the interview questions. Naturally, no one person could be expected to flawlessly answer all of the senior-level questions. Even the most adept DBAs have some areas of weakness.

In order to test the fairness of the questions, I asked numerous DBAs, from different backgrounds and companies, to review the questions. I was surprised by the results. Some questions that I thought were pretty easy were actually shown to be obscure (and therefore unfair.) Some reviewers suggested questions that at first I thought might be too difficult. In some cases, the reviewers thought a question was too difficult for that level, so it was moved to a higher level.

CLASSIFICATIONS

The need for performance tuning expertise suggests a separate classification. These questions are by nature more specific, but it seemed unfair to include them with the general questions. After all, not all firms are looking for performance tuners, so why penalize a candidate? Therefore, I have included a separate section just for performance tuning.

I have divided the interview questions into four categories, each having 25 questions:

- JUNIOR
- MIDDLE
- SENIOR
- PERFORMANCE-TUNING

SUGGESTIONS FOR INTERVIEWERS

Performing a fair interview is a bit of an art, but I have found these guidelines to be helpful:

- Start with the *junior* questions—even for those candidates who claim to be senior. This can save a lot of time[1]. It also sets qualified candidates at ease.
- Make it clear from the outset that *none* of the questions are trick questions designed to lure the candidate into saying a wrong answer. The "right" answer is likely the first one that comes into their head.

I Suggest you score the interview, with each answer receiving 0, 1 or ½ point. Thus, a perfect score would be 100%. Having a numerical score is very helpful when evaluating the strength of candidates. It also demonstrates that you have a consistent, fair process in place.

At the end of the interview, allow the candidate to ask about any questions on which they answered poorly. In explaining the correct answer, you may find that the question was misunderstood, or that you unintentionally misstated the question.

---

[1] For instance, if your candidate doesn't know what ORACLE_HOME means, you probably don't need to spend a lot of time in the *senior* category. (Actual situation.)

Remember that these interview questions are general in nature, but this may need suit all interviews. Depending on your firm's needs, you may need to add questions about features or applications critical to your company. For instance, you may need to add more detailed questions on backup methods, Pl/Sql, or talk about replication such as Streams.

I have found that truly qualified candidates actually enjoy answering fair questions—even when quite difficult. Most competent engineers enjoy showcasing their knowledge and to their qualifications. Furthermore, most people want to improve their knowledge and will want to correct their weaknesses.

I hope you find these 100 interview questions to be a fair and accurate way to assess the skill set of Oracle DBA candidates.

Christopher Lawson

JUNIOR DBA QUESTIONS

These 25 questions are applicable to DBAs with one or two year's actual hands-on experience. These questions are very simple and can be completed in about 10 minutes.

ON A UNIX SERVER, WHAT WOULD BE A TYPICAL VALUE FOR THE ENVIRONMENTAL VARIABLE, *ORACLE_HOME?*

On an OFA[2]-compliant setup, the following would be typical:

```
/u01/app/oracle/product/9.0.2
```

This is probably about the most basic question that can be asked of an Oracle DBA. The exact value is not important, nor is anyone required to be OFA compliant. For instance, instead of "/u01," there might be "/opt" or even "/oracle."

The important thing is that the candidate know what you mean by the question, and be able to state what setting they use.

For example, on a development server that I work on occasionally, here are the settings for two different databases:

```
/opt/oracle/product/9.2.0.8
/opt/oracle/product/10.2.0
```

---

[2] Optimal Flexible Architecture

WHAT'S THE OTHER KEY ENVIRONMENTAL PARAMETER THAT SPECIFIES THE DATABASE?

ORACLE_SID

It's difficult to accept any other answer except this one.

ON A UNIX SERVER, WHERE IS THE LISTENER.ORA FILE NORMALLY STORED?

This file is stored a few levels under ORACLE_HOME, in the /*network*/*admin* subdirectory. Here is one example:

```
/opt/oracle/product/10.2.0/network/admin
```

IF USERS CANNOT CONNECT TO THE DATABASE, HOW CAN YOU SEE IF THE LISTENER IS ACTUALLY RUNNING?

There are several acceptable answers here. The most obvious way is to issue the unix command, ***lsnrctl status.***

Another way is to look for the unix process running. If we were to issue the unix command, ***ps-ef***, we would see a process something like this:

```
/opt/oracle/product/10.2.0/bin/tnslsnr LISTENER
```

In the above line, *LISTENER* refers to the listener name (which can vary.)

Using a utility such as *tnsping* is not a very good answer, since we have already stated that users cannot connect to the database—that is, running tnsping doesn't really add useful information.

WHAT ARE SOME CRITICAL DRAWBACKS OF USING *EXPORT* AS THE SOLE BACKUP METHOD?

The most critical drawback is that a database recovery will be severely handicapped. If a database is restored from an export, your recovered database can only reflect the contents at the time the export was taken. That is, there will definitely be data loss. There will be no "rolling forward" of the database using the archive logs.

Another big drawback is that export tends to be unwieldy (and may be too slow) once the database grows very large.

DEFINE THE TERM "DRIVING TABLE"

This is a term related to table joins. The driving table is simply the one that the optimizer starts with first. The term applies regardless of the join method. Consider the following Sql:

```
Select * from Table1 T1, Table2 T2
Where T1.Id = T2.Id
And T1.Emp_First_Name = 'ALEXANDRA';
```

In this Sql, either Table1 or Table2 will be the driving table. (In our example, this will likely be Table1, because of the Emp_First_Name condition.)

The table that is *not* the driving table is called the "driven" table.

DEFINE THE TERM "FOREIGN KEY"

This is part of RI (Referential Integrity). A foreign key is the "child" entry that points to its parent. RI ensures that all children values also appear in the parent table.

HOW DOES A "CARTESIAN PRODUCT" HAPPEN?

A cartesian product is often a disastrous consequence performance wise. Although it is occasionally an intentional operation (such as between small tables), it most often occurs when the "Where" clause is accidentally omitted.

In the Sql below, we are missing the *Where* clause. Thus, Oracle will join every row in T1 to every row in T2—potentially yielding a huge result set.

```
Select * from Table1 T1, Table2 T2;
```

Cartesian products between two large tables may "never" complete the join, and the initiating session will likely need to be killed by the DBA.

WHAT ARE THE TWO MOST COMMON TYPES OF TABLE JOINS AND HOW DO THEY DIFFER?

The two are called *nested-loop* and *hash join*.

Nested-loop joins are often used when the result set is relatively small. Each row from the driving table that meets the extract criteria is matched, one at a time, to the corresponding row from the driven table.

A hash join, in contrast, is more appropriate when the result set is large. The driving table is scanned, with each row meeting the extract criteria assigned to a particular "bucket" using a hashing function applied to the join column.

Once the first table is processed, the same hashing function is applied to the rows in the second table. Rows that end up in the same bucket are candidates for joining because they likely (but not positively) have the same value for the join column.

WRITE A SQL WITH AN INLINE VIEW

Here's a simple example:

```
Select Emp_Id from Table1,
(Select Emp_id from Table2, Table3
Where Table2.Dept = Table3.Dept) VIEW1
Where Table1.Dept = VIEW1.Dept;
```

In the above Sql, *VIEW1* is an inline view.

WHAT IS A MATERIALIZED VIEW?

A materialized view is an object often used in data warehouses. It differs from a regular view in that the data is really populated with a materialized view. Thus, a materialized view has storage attributes and a specific number of rows. A regular view has no storage attributes.

A materialized view is often used to roll-up or summarize data for later retrieval.

WHY WOULD YOU EVER NEED A FUNCTION-BASED INDEX?

A function based index allows the optimizer to use an index even though some type of function has been applied.

```
Select count(*) from Big_Table
where Upper(Name) like 'Smith%';
```

In this Sql, an index on (Name) would not work because of the Upper function. A function index, on the other hand, would work well.

HOW DOES A DEADLOCK HAPPEN?

A deadlock occurs when two sessions are waiting for each other to complete their transaction. Consider the following:

SESSION 1

```
Update Emps set Emp_Id = 25;
```

SESSION 2

```
Update Boss_Name set Boss = 'Joe';
Update Emps set Emp_Id = 10;
```

At this point SESSION 2 is waiting for SESSION 1 to commit its changes to the Emps table.

Now, observe what would happen after this step:

SESSION 1

```
Update Boss_Name set Boss = 'Sam';
```

Now, SESSION 2 is still waiting to make its change to the Emps table, but now, SESSION 1 is waiting on the Boss_Name table.

This is a deadlock, since both sessions are stuck, and would remain so unless Oracle did something. In fact, Oracle rolls back one of the transactions with the error message,

ORA-00060: deadlock detected while waiting for resource

CONSIDER SHUTDOWN NORMAL/IMMEDIATE/ABORT—WHAT'S THE DIFFERENCE?

Shutdown Normal waits for all sessions to disconnect before proceeding. That's why it's not the first choice. Oracle writes out changes to the database files (i.e., performs a *checkpoint*.)

Shutdown Immediate waits for all transactions to complete (but users can still be connected.) Oracle performs a checkpoint of the database files.

Shutdown Abort waits for nothing. The database is shut down without regard to the users or ongoing transactions. The database files are not updated; this is not as bad as it sounds, since all relevant transactions are stored in the redo log.

HOW CAN YOU LIST ALL THE .DBF FILES USED FOR A PARTICULAR DATABASE?

A very easy way is to query DBA_DATA_FILES:

```
Select file_name from Dba_Data_Files;

/u/g11/03/oracle/proddb/system_01.dbf
/u/g13/02/oracle/proddb/undo_01.dbf
/u/g15/01/oracle/proddb/users_01.dbf
/u/g13/01/oracle/proddb/aud_01.dbf
/u/g11/04/oracle/proddb/emp_data1_01.dbf
```

WHERE DOES ORACLE TYPICALLY WRITE TRACE FILES?

They are written to the */udump* subdirectory.

HOW CAN YOU LIMIT RESOURCE USAGE FOR A CERTAIN GROUP OF USERS?

This is accomplished with an Oracle *Profile*. A profile is commonly used to restrict how many sessions a user may start, CPU time, connection time, etc.

DBA tools, such as Oracle Enterprise Manager (OEM) are often used to setup the profile restrictions, although using a GUI tool is not required to use profiles.

Query *DBA_PROFILES* to get a quick summary of the profile usage on your database.

WHAT'S AN EASY WAY TO IDENTIFY YOUR DATABASE VERSION?

There are several ways to do this. Probably the easiest is to start Sql*Plus, and observe the version number displayed. In the session below, the database version is 9.2.0.8.

```
SQL*Plus: Release 9.2.0.1.0 - Production on Thu
Nov 1 09:41:24 2007

Copyright (c) 1982, 2002, Oracle Corporation.
All rights reserved.

Connected to:
Oracle9i Enterprise Edition Release 9.2.0.8.0 -
64bit Production
        * * *
```

Another easy way is to query the view V$Version:

```
Select * from V$Version
where Banner like '%Database%'
```

BANNER

Oracle Database 10g Enterprise Edition Release
10.2.0.2.0 - 64bi

Here's yet another way:

```
Select Version from Product_Component_Version
where Product like '%Database%'
```

VERSION

10.2.0.2.0

DURING A HOT BACKUP WHAT CRITICAL STEP MUST BE PERFORMED BEFORE COPYING DATABASE FILES?

Each tablespace that is being backed-up must first be placed in backup mode. This is accomplished by issuing the command:

```
ALTER TABLESPACE [name] BEGIN BACKUP
```

Failure to perform this step (and the subsequence "End Backup") is a huge mistake and will result in an invalid backup.

HOW CAN YOU EASILY ESTIMATE THE NUMBER OF ROWS IN A TABLE WITHOUT RUNNING SELECT COUNT(*) ?

A simple way is to query DBA_TABLES (or USER_TABLES or ALL_TABLES). The estimate will be very good as long as statistics have been gathered recently.

```
Select Table_Name, Num_Rows from Dba_Tables
Where Table_Name like 'RETAIL%';
```

TABLE_NAME	NUM_ROWS
RETAIL_CUSTS	82376
RETAIL_MERCHANTS_HIST	90560

HOW CAN YOU EASILY SEE WHAT TEMPORARY TABLESPACE IS ASSIGNED TO A SPECIFIC USER?

The simplest way is to simply query DBA_USERS, like this:

```
Select Username, Temporary_Tablespace
from Dba_Users;

USERNAME         TEMPORARY_TAB
-------------    -------------
SYS              TEMP_PROD
SYSTEM           TEMP_PROD
DBSNMP           TEMP_PROD
ADMAPP           TEMP_PROD
JONES            TEMP_PROD
SMITH            TEMP_PROD
OUTLN            TEMP_PROD
```

HOW CAN YOU SEE IF YOUR DATABASE IS IN ARCHIVE LOG MODE?

There are several reasonable ways to accomplish this. Each is fine, and really is simply a matter of personal choice:

1) Here's the easiest: Simply ask the database!

```
Select Log_Mode from V$Database;

LOG_MODE
------------
ARCHIVELOG
```

2) Query V$Archived_Log and list recent archive logs:

```
Select Name,  First_Time, Next_time
from v$Archived_Log
where First_Time > Sysdate - 1;
```

3) As *SysDba*, run the following command:

```
SQL> Archive Log List

Database log mode             No Archive Mode
Automatic archival            Disabled
Archive destination
/u1/oracle/admin/db1/arch
Oldest online log sequence       95
Current log sequence            118
```

4) Of course, if you see lots of archive logs created recently on the server, this would also be proof (although that's not quite what we had in mind.)

WHAT WILL YOU SEE HAPPENING IF YOU KILL A SESSION THAT IS IN THE MIDDLE OF PERFORMING A GIANT TRANSACTION?

You will see the database rolling back—possibly for hours.

WHAT'S A HUGE DRAWBACK OF NOT USING ARCHIVE LOG MODE?

Your database recovery options will be severely limited. You will only be able to recover to your last full backup point. You will lose all transactions after that time.

WHAT FEATURE COULD ENSURE THAT A TABLESPACE WOULD NOT RUN OUT OF ROOM?

The *autoextend* feature allows Oracle to increase a database file size without DBA intervention. The DBA specifies the increment as well as the maximum allowable size for a particular .dbf file.

Although not necessarily suitable for all environments, autoextend is nonetheless a good option to have available.

MEDIUM-LEVEL QUESTIONS

These questions are applicable to DBAs with three to five year's actual hands-on experience. These questions should require about 20 minutes.

HOW CAN WE CHANGE OUR QUERY TO USE MORE RESOURCES TO SPEED-UP A FULL TABLE SCAN?

We can invoke Oracle parallelism. For instance, for a full scan, we can use the Parallel hint as follows:

```
Select /*+Parallel(T1 6) */
* from Table1 T1;
```

HOW DO YOU SEE ROLES GIVEN TO A USER?

An easy way is to query DBA_ROLE_PRIVS. In the following Sql, we check the roles given to "Bhanu."

```
Select Grantee, Granted_Role
from Dba_Role_Privs
Where Grantee = 'BHANU';

GRANTEE                        GRANTED_ROLE
------------------------       ---------------
BHANU                          CONNECT
BHANU                          DBA
BHANU                          RESOURCE
```

WHY DOES A "SNAPSHOT TOO OLD" ERROR OCCUR?

This is probably one of the most common interview questions. It's easy to see why. Understanding why this error occurs demonstrates a good grasp of some important Oracle concepts.

A user sees this error when the data needed for a long-running select is no longer available—it has been used for a new transaction. Thus, the snapshot of data is "too old," or more precisely, *doesn't exist*.

Oracle writes over an undo segment when the transaction using that area of undo has completed (committed or rolled-back). Unfortunately, Oracle is not smart enough to know that someone's *Select* statement still needs that data in order to preserve read consistency.

There are excellent ways to minimize the chances of this error (discussed in the next question.)

WHAT OPTIONS DO WE HAVE FOR PREVENTING A SNAPSHOT TOO OLD ERROR?

Prior to Oracle 9i, the usual measures were only partially effective. Typically, DBAs did the following:

- Try to run the long-running Select at a different time than other transactions operating on the same data
- Assign the offending transaction to a giant RBS segment using the *Set Transaction Use Rollback . . .* command.

Now, the DBA has much better tools to deal with this problem. The init.ora parameter *Undo_Retention* specifies how long Oracle should try to preserve an area in the Undo tablespace before it is overwritten. For example, a setting of 900 (seconds) means that Oracle will not overwrite an undo segment for 15 minutes (unless it is out of available undo space.)

Oracle 10g adds an interesting quirk. The Undo tablespace can be created with the option to *guarantee* the retention of undo areas—even if it causes some transactions to fail because there is no undo space!

The danger of using the guarantee option should be obvious; fortunately, the "guarantee" option is turned off by default. The guarantee option might conceivably be useful if you needed to ensure consistent behavior for "flashback" queries.

Here's how you see how a Undo tablespace has been configured:

```
Select Tablespace_Name, Retention
from Dba_Tablespaces
Where Tablespace_Name like 'UNDO%'

TABLESPACE_NAME                      RETENTION
------------------------------       -----------
UNDOTBS1                             NOGUARANTEE
```

HOW DOES ORACLE PRESERVE READ CONSISTENCY?

Oracle keeps multiple versions of a block as it is in the process of being changed by different users. Hence the name, *multiversion read consistency*.

Oracle needs to keep track of multiple block versions because each session is guaranteed to have a consistent view of the data—marked to the time of their initial access.

So, one session might need to go "backwards" just one version to retrieve data, whereas another session could conceivably need to go backwards hundreds or even thousands of steps to find a block of data as it existed when their query first began. So, a very simple query could conceivably take thousands of times longer than usual! (Incidentally, this is why we see performance degradation in a "hot" table.)

The "extra" block versions are kept in the undo tablespace.

WHAT'S ANOTHER NAME FOR A MATERIALIZED VIEW?

A *snapshot*.

DESCRIBE THE TWO BASIC WAYS TO REFRESH A MATERIALIZED VIEW.

You can do a *fast refresh*, or a *complete* refresh.

The fast refresh method is appropriate if you know that only a subset of the data has changed. Oracle uses a materialized view log to keep track of the changes so that only the "delta" needs to be applied.

On the other hand, if many rows in the underlying table have been modified, a *complete* refresh is probably the best choice.

WHAT ARE THE IMPORTANT LIMITATIONS OF GRANTING OBJECT PRIVILEGES VIA ROLES?

In most cases, an object privilege granted via a role works just fine. There is an important exception, however. When running a Pl/Sql procedure or function, the object privilege must have been granted *directly*—not via a role. Otherwise, Oracle will not be able to access the table, and the program will bomb.

To clarify, procedure owners (not executors) must be granted object privileges *directly*, rather than inheriting these through a role.

WHAT IS THE MAIN REASON TO INDEX FOREIGN KEYS?

This has nothing to do with performance; rather, this is a lock-avoidance issue. It is standard practice to put an index on all foreign keys if any transactions will be performed on the parent. Without an index, an update to a parent row will lock the child table.

Many difficult-to-diagnose locking issues have arisen because of forgetting this practice.

DESCRIBE A MAJOR FUNCTIONALITY PROBLEM WITH BIT-MAP INDEXES

Bit-map indexes are almost always avoided on OLTP systems because of severe locking issues.

Normally, Oracle simply locks the row that is being updated. This is well-known behavior. With a bitmap index, however, many rows (but usually not all) can be locked at one time—even if only one row is being updated! Naturally, this can lead to horrific locking problems and user delays.

These types of indexes can also cause performance degradation, but that is not as significant as the locking problems.

WHAT'S THE ADVANTAGE OF USING *PGA AGGREGATE TARGET* ?

In the past, a user would be strictly limited on the amount of hashing space or sorting area that they could consume. This was based on the init.ora parameters, Sort_Area_Size and Hash_Area_Size.

With a PGA target, on the other hand, Oracle dynamically allocates more space to an individual session—as long as there is space available. This new method is potentially superior, since sessions that need more space can automatically get it (up to certain limits.)

The controlling init.ora parameters are:

- Workarea_Size_Policy
- PGA_Aggregate_Target

IN PERFORMING A DATABASE RECOVERY, WHAT'S THE SIGNIFICANCE OF "RESETLOGS?"

This option marks a "point of no-return" in database recovery, and should be used with extreme care. The actual command is:

```
Alter Database Open ResetLogs
```

When a DBA specifies ResetLogs, it means that Oracle will re-initialize the transaction (redo) log—so that no further recovery is possible.[3]

For instance, if the DBA is "rolling forward" the database, applying various archive logs, issuing *resetlogs* will make further application of archive logs *impossible*.

The resetlogs option is commonly used when cloning a database, in which the DBA has provided new locations for the .dbf files, and has re-created the control file.

---

[3] Technically, there are some exceptions to this, especially since Oracle 10gR2.

43

ON A UNIX SERVER, HOW CAN YOU SPECIFY A DIFFERENT DIRECTORY FOR THE *LISTENER.ORA* FILE?

This is done using the UNIX environment variable, *TNS_ADMIN*.

HOW CAN ORACLE AUTOMATICALLY CHECK FOR OBSOLETE STATISTICS?

When gathering statistics with the *Dbms_Stats* package, you can use the option, "GATHER STALE." With this option, Oracle will only update statistics on those tables that have been modified by more than 10%.

An important prerequisite to this feature is that you must first activate table monitoring (one-time step), so that Oracle can recognize how tables have changed. (Note, however, that table monitoring is on by default in later Oracle versions.)

You can enable monitoring for a single table, an entire schema, or even the entire database. Here's an example for a single table:

```
Alter Table Chris1 Monitoring;
```

In this example we monitor an entire schema:

```
Exec Dbms_Stats.Alter_Schema_Table_Monitoring
('LAWSON', TRUE);
```

Once monitoring has been activated, here's how we would update stats for those tables having stale information:

```
Exec Dbms_Stats.Gather_Schema_Stats( -
ownname          => 'LAWSON', -
options          => 'GATHER STALE')
```

There are actually two related options that you may consider:

- Gather *Stale*: Update statistics if there have been at least 10% modifications.

- Gather *Auto*: Same as Stale, except also get new statistics on those objects having no statistics.

Since you normally want statistics on all tables, the *Gather Auto* appears to be the better choice for most applications.

WHY WOULD I EVER USE A GLOBAL TEMPORARY TABLE, INSTEAD OF A REGULAR TABLE?

The usual reason for using a global temporary table, instead of a "regular" table is this: Different sessions require some type of temporary staging table, and it is needed just for the duration of the session.

By using a global temporary table, there is no possibility of locking conflicts, since each session gets its own version of the table.

There is a further advantage, in that transactions on a global temporary table generally produce less redo than transactions on a "regular" table.

HOW CAN I CHANGE HOW MANY BLOCKS ORACLE READS AT A SINGLE TIME?

The parameter is called, *Db_File_MultiBlock_Read_Count*. It is an *init.ora* parameter, that we typically set once for the entire database.

In addition, it can be set for a particular session, using

```
Alter Session
Set Db_File_Multiblock_Read_Count = 128;
```

For a database that has both OLTP and large batch jobs performing full scans, it is common to change this setting at the start of the batch job.

We discuss what value to use for this parameter in a later question, in the *Performance Tuning* section.

WHAT'S AN EASY WAY TO CHECK THE VALUE OF A PARTICULAR INIT.ORA PARAMETER?

There are several good ways:

- In Sql*Plus, issue the command, *Show Parameter [parname]*
- Run a query on the view, *V$System_Parameter*, or *V$Parameter*, like this:

```
Select Name, Value
from V$Parameter
where upper(Name) like '%PGA%'
```

```
NAME                             VALUE
-------------------------------- ------------
pga_aggregate_target             4194304000
```

HOW CAN YOU IDENTIFY WHAT QUERIES OR TRANSACTIONS ARE RUNNING IN THE DATABASE RIGHT NOW?

You can join the views V$Session and V$Sql. There are many different possibilities for field selection—here is one example:

```
Select DISTINCT Sid, Username,
Substr(Sql_Text,1,200) Stext
From V$Session, V$Sql
Where Status = 'ACTIVE'
And Username Is Not Null
And V$Session.Sql_Hash_Value = Hash_Value
And V$Session.Sql_Address  = V$Sql.Address
And Sql_Text Not Like '%Sql_Text%'
And Username <> 'SYS';
```

In the above query, we eliminate the SYS user because we don't want to clutter up the output with information about the Oracle background processes. Also, we exclude Sql that includes the phrase, "Sql_Text" because otherwise this very Sql will show up as active.

HOW CAN YOU USE A SQL HINT SO AS TO CHANGE THE JOIN ORDER?

There are several good ways.

Firstly, you can use the *Leading* sql hint to specify the leading table. In the following sql, we want *Table1* to start the join:

```
Select /*+Leading(T1) */
* from Table1 T1, Table2 T2
where T1.Emp_Id = T2.Emp_Id
and T1.Name like '%Smith%'
and T2.Dept like '%Engineering%';
```

Alternatively, you can use the *Ordered* hint, which, together with the order of tables in the *from* clause, specifies the join order for all the tables. In the following sql, we want Table2 to start the join, so we put it first after the keyword *from*.

```
Select /*+Ordered*/
* from Table2 T2, Table1 T1
where T1.Emp_Id = T2.Emp_Id
and T1.Name like '%Smith%'
and T2.Dept like '%Engineering%';
```

IN THE EXPORT UTILITY, WHAT DOES THE OPTION, "COMPRESS" MEAN?

It simply means that upon import, all the extents of an object are put into (i.e., "compressed") a single extent.

Using this option can be troublesome, since there may not be enough contiguous space for Oracle to actually force all the extents into one.

GIVE AN EXAMPLE OF A "SET OPERATION."
WHY WOULD I NEED TO USE A SET OPERATION?

Set operations include

- **MINUS**
- **INTERSECT**
- **UNION**
- **UNION ALL**

These are commonly used when the result set requires manipulating large groups of data. For example, if you needed to find the rows that satisfy one query, but are *not* included in another, you could use the MINUS operation. (For large result sets, this is often a better choice than the *not in* syntax.)

Other examples would be finding the *common* rows using INTERSECT, or finding the rows in *either* query using UNION or UNION ALL. (UNION differs from UNION ALL in that the duplicates are removed in the former operation.)

FOR A LONG-RUNNING TABLE SCAN, HOW COULD I EASILY SEE THE PROGRESS?

Oracle Enterprise Manager (OEM) has a very nice graphic that shows the progress. Hopefully, we DBAs can investigate even without having a good GUI tool handy.

Behind the scenes, OEM is actually querying a view called *V$Session_Longops*.

Here is one possible way to query the view, *V$Session_Longops*, assuming we are interested in session 123:

```
Select Sid, Message
from V$Session_Longops
where Sid = 123;

   SID MESSAGE
 ----- ------------------------------------------------
  2057 Table Scan:  CHRIS.TABLEX: 926717 out of 926717
       Blocks done
```

Here's a slight different way to accomplish the same thing:

```
Select Sid, Time_Remaining, Elapsed_Seconds
from V$Session_Longops
where Sid = 123;

   SID TIME_REMAINING ELAPSED_SECONDS
 ----- -------------- ---------------
   123             11              58
```

IF YOU FORGOT THE EXACT NAME OF A CERTAIN V$VIEW, HOW COULD YOU FIND IT?

There are several views that have this information. Here are a few possibilities:

- DBA_Views
- DBA_Objects

For example, if we forgot the exact name of the "long ops" view, we could do this:

```
Select View_Name from DBA_Views
where
View_Name like 'V%LONG%';

VIEW_NAME
--------------------
V_$SESSION_LONGOPS
V_$AW_LONGOPS
```

The above results suggest there must be a synonym that doesn't have the "_" character, so we now check for that:

```
Select Synonym_Name
from DBA_Synonyms
where Synonym_Name like '%V$%LONG%'

SYNONYM_NAME
-----------------------------
V$SESSION_LONGOPS
V$AW_LONGOPS
GV$SESSION_LONGOPS
GV$AW_LONGOPS
```

As expected, the name of the view is simply, *V$Session_Longops*.

HOW CAN YOU TELL WHEN A TABLE WAS LAST ANALYZED?

Simply query *DBA_Tables* and retrieve the column *Last_Analyzed*:

```
Select Table_Name, Last_Analyzed
from DBA_Tables
where Table_Name = `EMP';

TABLE_NAME                      LAST_ANAL
------------------------------- ---------
EMP                             22-NOV-06
```

WHY DO WE CARE IF BIND VARIABLES ARE USED BY AN APPLICATION?

Generally speaking, we don't want to issue huge numbers of distinct Sql statements, because each one requires a new "hard" parse by the Oracle optimizer. Oracle recognizes that the statement does not yet exist in the shared pool, and has to start from scratch in parsing and building an execution plan.

True, it's typically only a small amount of additional cpu time; the problem is when this oversight extends to many thousands or millions of individual Sql, at which point the extra time quickly becomes significant.

SENIOR-LEVEL QUESTIONS

These questions are applicable to DBAs with over five year's actual hands-on experience. These questions can be fully answered in about 20 minutes.

Keep in mind that we are typically not interested in the precise syntax or spelling of any answer. No applicant should be penalized based on such mundane criteria.

GIVE AN EXAMPLE OF A *SCALAR SUBQUERY*

A scalar subquery, a recent addition to Oracle, is a subquery that returns exactly one column value from one row. This feature can be very powerful, but can also be confusing for other developers to follow.

Whereas an inline view is a select statement embedded in the *from* clause, a scalar subquery is a select statement embedded in the *select* clause.

For example, if we wanted to list each part in a table, along with the distance to its nearest location, we could run this scalar subquery:

```
Select
(Select Min(Distance) From Parts P1
where P1.Part_name = P2.Part_name) Min_Distance,
Part_Name
From Parts P2
```

In the above Sql, the code to find *Min_Distance* is the scalar subquery.

A scalar subquery will oftentimes employ a function such as *Min* or *Max*. This is understandable since by definition a scalar subquery is not allowed to return more than one row.

HOW DO YOU LIMIT THE MAXIMUM NUMBER OF PARALLEL PROCESSES FOR THE DATABASE?

This is an init.ora parameter:

```
Parallel_Max_Servers
```

WHAT ARE TYPICAL WAYS TO PARTITION A TABLE?

Your choices are:

- *List partitioning:* Distributes data to partitions based on explicit pre-determined values, such as factory names, or geographical regions.
- *Range partitioning:* Commonly based on a range of dates. It is very common to have monthly partitioning.
- *Hash partitioning:* Used when data needs to be spread evenly across partitions, without using any particular business model.

In recent versions of Oracle, you have two new options:

- *Interval partitioning:* Similar to range partitioning, but used for equi-partitioned tables whereby Oracle automatically creates partitions as needed. A typical use would be for *monthly* partitions.
- *Reference partitioning:* A child table inherits the partitioning strategy of the parent table, without the need to store the partition key in the child table.

A more complex method, called *composite* partitioning, is discussed in the next question.

WHY WOULD WE EVER NEED TO USE *COMPOSITE* PARTITIONS?

With composite partitioning, data is subdivided even further. If the data sets are extremely large, this may further improve performance by further reducing the data that is considered.

There is also a potential benefit if your application requires hash joins of large data sets. (See the first option, below.)

Common choices for composite partitioning are:

Range-Hash: The data is first distributed based on the range of the partition key—such as a monthly partition. Each range partition is then subdivided based on hashing of the subpartition key. This method is especially helpful if there are hash-joins that will take place between the subpartitions. Instead of hash joining all the data in a particular range, Oracle is able to hash-join each subpartition to its counterpart—that is, one subpartition joins to one subpartition.

Range-List: After the initial division based on range, the data is further segmented based on an explicit list.

Depending on your version of Oracle, it may also be possible to use one of these forms of composite partitioning:

- Range-Range
- List-List
- List-Range
- List-Hash
- Interval-List
- Interval-Hash
- Interval-Range.

WHAT'S THE DIFFERENCE BETWEEN A *GLOBAL* INDEX AND A *LOCAL* INDEX?

A local index means that the index partitioning method *matches* the table partitioning method. So, if the table has 20 partitions based on the range of a particular column, the index will also have 20 partitions based on range.

A global index means that the index partitioning method is *independent* of the underlying table's method. The global index can be either *Global Partitioned* or *Global Non-Partitioned*.

In practical usage, we often use the term global index to mean that the index is not partitioned at all (i.e., the global *non-partitioned* variety.) Technically speaking, however, a global index is not restricted to just that one form.

Each type of index has its usefulness, especially in performance tuning. Of special concern is whether a typical query includes the partition key in the *where* clause.

WHAT PROBLEM USUALLY OCCURS ON A GLOBAL INDEX IF WE RUN DDL ON THE TABLE? CAN THIS PROBLEM BE AVOIDED?

If we perform a DDL operation on a partitioned table, a global index will typically be marked *Invalid*, and it must be rebuilt. An example of such an operation would be dropping one of the partitions.

The global index issue can be avoided by using the clause, *Update Global Indexes* at the time you perform *DDL*. For example:

```
Alter Table Emps Truncate Partition Sept_07
Update Global Indexes;
```

HOW CAN WE IDENTIFY UNUSED INDEXES?

You can use *index monitoring*. Oracle provides a monitoring facility whereby you can see if an index is ever used during the monitoring period. The command to start monitoring is really simple. For instance, if we want to monitor the index *Chris1*, we run the following:

```
Alter Index Chris1 Monitoring Usage;
```

After several days (or weeks), check the results by running:

```
Select Index_Name, Table_Name, Used
From V$Object_Usage;

INDEX_NAME          TABLE_NAME            USED
----------------    --------------------  ---
CHRIS1              CHRISTEST             NO
```

To turn off monitoring, simply run:

```
Alter Index Chris1 Nomonitoring Usage;
```

While useful, this simple "Yes"/"No" answer for each index checked is not that helpful. It would be much more useful to identify the exact SQL that used the index, along with the resource usage.

For example, Oracle might be using a certain index only because you haven't given it any better alternatives. Just because the index is used, doesn't mean it's a good choice. By knowing statistics such as elapsed time or disk i/o, you can identify tuning opportunities.

WHEN DOES AN IMPLICIT COMMIT OCCUR?

Oracle issues an *implicit commit* whenever you run a DDL command. In other words, every DDL that you run is really assigned a separate transaction.

This is not normally an issue—unless you expect to perform a rollback, or control the commits for some business reason. Note that when you execute the DDL transaction, issuing a subsequent *Rollback* or *Commit* command will do nothing.

For example, suppose you perform the following update:

```
Update Chris_Test
set object_name = 'TESTER';
```

Now, if you execute the following DDL command (on a completely unrelated object), your changes to Chris_Test will be implicitly committed:

```
Truncate Table Test-Table;
```

Here's another example of DDL that will cause your changes to commit:

```
Create Table Test_Table2 As
Select * From User_Objects;
```

Once again, note that the table affected by the DDL command can be *completely unrelated* to your initial changes.

WHAT IS THE PURPOSE OF AN *AUTONOMOUS TRANSACTION?*

Normally, a job that is performing a series of transactions wants them all to either commit or rollback together. Sometimes, however, it is necessary for one of the transactions to commit or rollback *independently* of the others. The transaction that is separate is called an autonomous transaction.

One example would be auditing of important financial transactions. A batch program might want all changes to be logged into some sort of audit table, regardless of whether the other transactions done at the same time were cancelled. The procedure performing the autonomous transaction must either commit or rollback before exiting.

An autonomous transaction is indicated by the presence of the phrase,

```
Pragma Autonomous Transaction
```

Here is an example:

```
Procedure Auto_Test
Is
   Pragma Autonomous_Transaction;
Begin
    Update TableX ...
    Commit;
End Auto_Test;
```

IS IT POSSIBLE TO TURN OFF LOGGING FOR ALL TRANSACTIONS IN THE DATABASE?

No, that is not possible. Only certain operations may be excluded.

The exact transactions that can be excluded from logging are discussed in the next question.

GIVE AN EXAMPLE OF A TYPE OF OPERATION THAT CAN EXCLUDE LOGGING

There are only a small number of operations that can exclude logging. Here are some common examples:

```
Create Index
Alter Index Rebuild
SQL*Loader Direct Path Load
Direct Path Insert
Create Table As Select
```

Some other (much more rare) operations include:

```
Alter Table Move [or Split]
Alter Index Split Partition
```

Of course, no one person should be expected to have all these types of operations memorized. The key point is that there are just a handful of operations that can preclude logging.

WHAT'S THE DANGER OF USING THE NOLOGGING OPTION FOR A TRANSACTION?

Using *Nologging* can be a hazardous step on an important production database. Here's why: If a transaction is not logged, then certain objects may be missed if the database subsequently crashes, and a recovery is performed. Specifically, the changes will be at risk until a database backup is performed.

For example, suppose we create a new index called *Indexnew* using the *Nologging* option. Until the database files containing that index are backed up (using either a cold or hot backup), *Indexnew* will simply not exist in either the redo logs or the database backup. If it doesn't exist in the redo logs, that means that Oracle will not re-create it when rolling forward the recovery.

The point is that a missing object may have disastrous consequences for your application. The DBA would simply have to *remember* to restore any object created using Nologging.

WHY DOES "ITL" LOCKING OCCUR?

ITL stands for *Interested Transaction List*. This type of locking occurs when many sessions are trying to update the same block, but there is no more room in the header to account for more transactions. When ITL locking occurs, the latest transaction will wait until one of the earlier transactions commits or rolls back, thereby freeing up an ITL slot.

ITL locking is a bit rare, but occasionally happens—usually in environments running complex batch jobs. When this occurs it can be extremely frustrating, since the symptoms closely resemble row-level locking.

Several things have to happen at the same time to get an ITL lock:

- Multiple sessions try to update the exact same block
- There are no more ITL slots in the header block
- There is no spare room in the data block to allow header to expand (i.e., the block is jammed full.)

Oracle typically reserves two ITL slots in the block header. This is configurable, and is controlled by the parameter, *Initrans*, set when the table is first created.

You can detect ITL waits in your database by querying the view, *V$Segment_Statistics*. Here's one example:

```
Select Owner,
Object_Name||' '||Subobject_Name Object_Name,
Value
From V$Segment_Statistics
Where Statistic_Name = 'ITL waits'
And Value > 0
Order By 3,1,2;
```

HOW CAN I SEE WHAT OBJECT IS BEING READ BY A CERTAIN SESSION AT THE PRESENT TIME?

The easiest way, available since Oracle 9i, is to query the *V$Sql* view and look for the column *Dba_Object_Id*. You join that to Dba_Objects to get the table (or index) name.

Here's one possibility, which shows the username, the sql being run, and the actual object name currently being read:

```
Select DISTINCT Osuser, Sid, Username,
Substr(Program,1,19) PROG, Object_Name,
Sql_Text
From V$Session, V$Sql, Dba_Objects O
Where V$Session.Status = 'ACTIVE'
And Username Is Not Null
And O.Object_Id = Row_Wait_Obj#
And V$Session.Sql_Hash_Value = Hash_Value
And V$Session.Sql_Address  = V$Sql.Address
And Username <> 'SYS';
```

In the above sql, I eliminate Sys users, since I'm typically interested in regular users, not some DBA (or background) activity.

Another valid way (but much more cumbersome), is to use wait events. Using *V$Session_Wait* and the p1,p2,p3 parameters, you first determine the file number and block. You then figure out what object matches that file/block combination. This older method works, but of course takes much longer. (This second method applies only to reading from *disk*.)

HOW CAN I SUMMARIZE THE CUMULATIVE RESOURCES USED BY A PARTICULAR SESSION?

If the session is your *own* session, than you can use the view, *V$Mystat*. This view includes cumulative values for many different actions:

```
Select Name, Value
From V$Mystat One, V$Statname Two
Where One.Statistic# = Two.Statistic#
And Value > 50000;
```

NAME	VALUE
physical read total bytes	237568
physical read bytes	237568

If the statistics are for some *other* session, you can use the view, *V$sesstat*:

```
Select Sid, Name, Value From V$Sesstat One,
V$Statname Two
Where Sid = 592
And One.Statistic# = Two.Statistic#
And Value > 5000000;
```

SID	NAME	VALUE
592	physical read total bytes	273842176
592	physical read bytes	273842176

In the above sql, we just wanted to see activity exceeding a certain threshold. You will likely want to exclude some resource usage—perhaps things like connect time, or bytes transferred over Sql*net. Of course, we could have instead focused on some particular resource. For example, we could show physical i/o using this:

```
Select Sid, Name, Value From V$Sesstat One,
V$Statname Two
Where Sid = 592
And One.Statistic# = Two.Statistic#
And Upper(Name) like '%PHYSICAL READS';
```

HOW CAN I MAKE ALL MY COMMANDS DEFAULT TO A DIFFERENT SCHEMA?

This is really easy, using the Alter *Session* command:

```
Alter Session Set Current_Schema = Joe;
```

Now, every command will act as though you have qualified the object name with "Joe."

WHAT IS *QUERY SUBFACTORING* AND WHY IS IT HELPFUL?

This is sometimes called the "With" syntax, because that's exactly how the Sql begins. Query subfactoring is very similar to using an inline view, except that the subfactor is put at the very front of the query. Then, the main body of your sql can read from it, just like a view.

This syntax is often used to make a complicated query more readable. In many cases, you could use inline views instead, but that would likely be more cumbersome for others to review.

Here's an example of query subfactoring:

```
With Part1 as
(Select * from Emp
Where Emp_Name like '%SMITH%')
(Select Count(*)
from Part1);
```

In this simple example, *Part1* is the subfactor. Although this example only has a single subfactor (*Part1*), you can include many subfactors up front (but you don't repeat the *With* keyword)

When you use query subfactoring, Oracle may either temporarily store the subfactor data in a global temporary table, or it may re-retrieve the data each time it is needed. This can have a big performance impact, especially on a very busy OLTP system, so you may need to carefully test each method. (You can see when Oracle builds a global temp table in the trace file.)

You can control how the optimizer handles the subfactor with these sql hints:

- *Inline*: Extract the data each time it is needed.
- *Materialize*: Gather the data once and store.

HOW CAN PARALLEL PROCESSES BE WORKING ON A QUERY, EVEN THOUGH NO SQL HINT WAS SPECIFIED?

Sometimes the DBA will set parallelism at the table (or index) level. This is probably not a great idea, but it happens.

Here is an easy way to see if parallelism is set at the table level:

```
Select Table_Name, Degree
from Dba_Tables
where Degree not like '%1%';
```

And to check indexes:

```
Select Index_Name, Degree
from Dba_Indexes
where Degree not like '%1%';
```

Very often, after rebuilding an index in parallel, the DBA will forget to reset the index back to Noparallel.

WHAT MIGHT BE WRONG WITH SETTING PARALLELISM AT THE TABLE (OR INDEX) LEVEL?

The problem is that you lose control over exactly when parallelism is used. If you set parallelism at the table or index level, Oracle will attempt to start parallel processes anytime you include the table in your query. This means that you will be taking away resources that might have been better used servicing other transactions and queries.

Depending on the exact sql, the parallel processes may not actually begin, but why take the chance? In actuality, you probably only wanted parallelism for a specific type of query—not for *all* queries on that table.

WHAT PARAMETER MUST BE SET FOR FUNCTION-INDEXES TO BE USED?

You must enable *query rewrite*. This is typically done at the database level, but you can also change it at the session level, using *Alter Session* . . .

Technically, there are two parameters involved, typically set as follows:

- QUERY_REWRITE_ENABLED=TRUE
- QUERY_REWRITE_INTEGRITY=TRUSTED

Note: The query-rewrite requirement was eliminated after Oracle 9.2.0.4.

HOW CAN YOU SEE WHICH SESSIONS ARE ACTIVE?

The easiest way is to look at *V$Session*, and retrieve only the sessions having Status = 'ACTIVE.'

Here's one easy way to show the active sessions and the sql they are running at present time:

```
Select DISTINCT OSUSER, Sid, Username,
Substr(Program,1,19) PROG ,
Substr(Sql_Text,1,200) Stext
From V$Session, V$Sql
Where Status = 'ACTIVE'
And Username Is Not Null
And V$Session.Sql_Hash_Value = Hash_Value
And V$Session.Sql_Address  = V$Sql.Address
And Sql_Text Not Like '%Sql_Text%'
And Username <> 'SYS';
```

In the above sql, we eliminate *SYS* users, as well as users running sql containing the phrase, 'Sql_Text' – because that would be us!

WHAT DOES IT MEAN WHEN ORACLE INDICATES THAT A SESSION IS "ACTIVE?"

It means that the session is actively doing work *at that very moment*.

For example, an active session is oftentimes doing disk i/o, but that is not the only reason to be active. The session might be performing a complex join and consuming lots of CPU.

Very often, especially on OLTP systems, such as customer service applications, nearly all of the sessions are *inactive*. This simply reflects the fact that most of the user's time is spent doing something else, such as talking to a customer on the phone, or typing in a request. The actual database request usually completes in a fraction of a second.

Active does *not* just mean that the user is connected to Oracle.

PERFORMANCE TUNING QUESTIONS

I have included performance tuning as a separate section, because the questions must be far more specific than general DBA questions. That is, it would be unfair to focus an interview on performance tuning, if your needs don't really require this expertise.

These questions are applicable to DBAs with at least three years performance tuning experience.

WHAT IS A *BUFFER_BUSY* WAIT AND WHY DOES IT HAPPEN?

There's a few different ways for this wait event to occur. A buffer busy wait happens because one session needs a block, but another session is in the process of reading it from disk. This is a wait that often occurs when there is a large amount of physical i/o.

Another common way to experience this wait event is due to *freelist contention*, for databases not using ASSM (Automatic Segment Space Management.)

Objects that are experiencing a large number of buffer busy waits can be identified by querying the view, *V$Segment_Statistics*. Here is one example:

```
Select Owner,
Object_Name||' '||Subobject_Name Object_Name,
Value
From V$Segment_Statistics
Where Statistic_Name Like '%busy%'
And Value > 990000
Order By 4,2,3;
```

OWNER	OBJECT_NAME	VALUE
CHRIS	EMP_NAMES	50089

In the above sql, we just retrieve those objects having a very large number of buffer busy waits.

WITHOUT STATSPACK REPORTS, HOW CAN I IDENTIFY THE OBJECTS INCURRING THE MOST LOGICAL & PHYSICAL READS?

Of course, this information is available on Statspack and AWR reports. If you don't have these reports available, one easy way is to query the view, *V$Segment_Statistics*.

Here is one example for finding objects with huge logical i/o:

```
Select Owner,Statistic_Name,
Object_Name||' '||Subobject_Name Object_Name,
Value
From V$Segment_Statistics
Where Statistic_Name Like '%logical reads%'
And Value > 333000000
Order By 4,2,3;
```

OWNER	STATISTIC_NAME	OBJECT_NAME	VALUE
CHRIS	logical reads	TEST_TABLE	368389216

Here's an example for physical reads:

```
Select Owner,Statistic_Name,
Object_Name||' '||Subobject_Name Object_Name,
Value
From V$Segment_Statistics
Where Statistic_Name Like '%physical reads%'
And Value > 333000000
Order By 4,2,3;
```

OWNER	STATISTIC_NAME	OBJECT_NAME	VALUE
CHRIS	physical reads	TEST_TABLE	561526416

Naturally, you will customize your query to fit your own system.

WHAT'S THE DIFFERENCE BETWEEN *SEQUENTIAL* AND *SCATTERED* READS?

- A sequential read is a *single-block* read.

- A scattered read is a *multi-block* read.

OLTP systems typically have large amounts of sequential reads, since most queries use efficient indexes, and just retrieve a few blocks of data for each query.

Batch jobs will often perform scattered reads, since full table scans are much more common.

WHAT'S A TYPICAL RATE THAT ORACLE CAN PERFORM SEQUENTIAL READS?

Single block reads are typically performed at rates above 100/sec. On many systems, the rate can be above 200 seq reads/sec.

In the next question, we address how to discover the rate on a particular database.

HOW CAN YOU ESTIMATE THE *SEQUENTIAL READ RATE* ACHIEVABLE BY A SINGLE SESSION?

There are several good ways to do this. In a given Statspack or AWR report, sequential reads are listed. Very often, sequential reads will be listed as part of the "Top 5 Timed Events."

Even if sequential reads are not a "top 5" event, this information will be listed, along with all wait events, in the "Wait Event" section. In this section, the average wait (ms) is shown. Simply take the reciprocal to get the read rate.

Besides reports, you can easily estimate the rate achievable (for a single thread) by querying a view such as *V$FileStat*, or *V$System_Event*. Here's one possibility:

```
Select EVENT, TOTAL_WAITS,  TIME_WAITED ,
Round(100*Total_Waits/Time_Waited) Rate
From V$System_Event
Where Event Like 'db file sequential read%';
```

EVENT	TOTAL_WAITS	TIME_WAITED	RATE
db file sequential read	6232709774	226760222	274

Note that the rate above is an estimate of what a *single* thread could reasonably achieve.

Another possibility is to examine the appropriate wait event in a tkprof output. This will not be as accurate, however, since the listing shows the wait times just for the particular session being traced, rather than an overall rate for a long period of time.

HOW CAN YOU FIND THE EXECUTION PATH THAT WAS *ACTUALLY RUN?*

This question is not as trivial as it may appear. The key here is understanding that the results of an *Explain Plan* are not necessarily the same as the plan *actually run*. Of course, the vast majority of times, the explain plan is very accurate—but not always!

The execution plan that was actually run in the database is available in the view, *V$Sql_Plan*. You can query this table just like the usual Plan_Table. The difference is, that you identify the sql a little differently.

Here's one way to do it: First, find the address for the sql in question. This is listed in the view, *V$Sql*. Then, simply query V$Sql_Plan using that address.

Here's an example:

```
Select Cost, Object_Name, Operation, Options
From V$Sql_Plan
Where Address = '00000005fc1e1998';
```

COST	OBJECT_NAME	OPERATION	OPTIONS
31		SELECT STATEMENT	
		COUNT	STOPKEY
31		VIEW	
31		SORT	ORDER BY STOPKEY
30		PARTITION RANGE	ALL
30	EMP_HIST	TABLE ACCESS	BY LOCAL INDEX ROWID
29	EMP_IDX1	INDEX	RANGE SCAN

HOW CAN TABLE PARTITIONING ACTUALLY *HURT* PERFORMANCE?

Depending on the exact queries that are executed, it is very possible that queries on partitioned tables will run worse than a non-partitioned table. Although people are often surprised by this result, it is not at all unusual. In fact, one of the main tasks when partitioning tables is to ensure against this possibility.

The key point is this: Is the partitioning key contained in the *where* clause? If not, the optimizer will not be able to restrict the scope of work to just a few partitions. That is, *partition pruning* will not occur.

Depending on the type of indexes (local versus global), this can have a terrible performance impact. Consider a very large table, Emp_*History*, which has been partitioned into 52 weekly partitions (based on employee start date.). Now look at the query below:

```
Select *
from Emp_History
where Dept = 101;
```

In the above query, Oracle can use a local index on *Dept*. However, the *where* clause does not include the partition key. So, if the local index on Dept is used, Oracle has no choice but to scan *all 52 partitions*. Without partitioning, the same query would have resulted in only 1 index range scan.

WHAT ARE THE P1,P2,P3 PARAMETERS?

These are *wait event parameters*. When using Oracle's wait event facility, they provide extra information for the particular wait event.

For example, here's a sql to retrieve the sequential read wait event— probably one of the most common wait events.

```
Select Sid, Event, P1, P2, P3
From V$Session_Wait
Where Event Like '%db file seq%';
```

SID	EVENT	P1	P2	P3
1998	db file sequential	12	564683	1
821	db file sequential	12	403592	1

In the sql above, P1 represents the file#, P2 represents the block id, and P3 indicates how many Oracle blocks were read. Of course, the P1-P3 parameters have different interpretations for different wait events.

Note that the event names are listed in *V$Event_Name*.

WHAT SQL HINT IS USED FOR A HASH JOIN?

The hint is *USE_HASH*.

For example,

```
Select /*+Use_Hash (T1 T2) */
Emp_Number
from Table1 T1, Table2 T2
where T1.Name like 'Johnson'
and T1.Id = T2.Id.;
```

WHAT'S AN EASY WAY TO SEE HOW MUCH DISK I/O WAS USED BY A SQL STATEMENT?

There's several ways to accomplish this. Probably the easiest (and fastest) way is to simply look at the view, *V$Sql*, and examine the column *Disk_Reads*. Here's an example:

```
Select Executions EXEC, Buffer_Gets GETS,
Disk_Reads IO, Sql_Text
From V$Sql
Where Upper(Sql_Text) Like '%EMP_TABLE%';

  EXEC    GETS      IO SQL_TEXT
------- ------- ------- --------------------------
     2       2      99 Select * from Emp_Table
```

We should note that this V$Sql view provides *cumulative* statistics. Therefore, if more than one user is running the identical sql, the results will be larger than for just a single user.

Of course, the same statistical information is also available in the Statspack and AWR reports, but it's often faster to just query V$Sql to get the same information.

Another way is to trace a session, then review the trace output.

WHAT SETTING SHOULD I USE FOR
DB_FILE_MULTIBLOCK_READ_COUNT?

Most commonly, a Unix server can read up to 1 Mb at a time. We then set the value of Db_File_MultiBlock_Read_Count so that:

```
Db_File_MultiBlock_Read_Count x Db_Block_Size = 1Mb.
```

Using a common size of 8k block size, we thus would set the multiblock value to 128.

If you're not sure of the maximum block read for your server, here's one easy way to check the limit:

1) In a Sql*Plus session, use *Alter Session* to crank up the value of Db_File_MultiBlock_Read_Count to a huge value (e.g., 500).
2) Start a long-running table scan in that session.
3) In another session, use Oracle's Wait Event facility to watch how many blocks are ever read at one time by the other session. This will be the "p3" parameter in the view V$Session_Wait.

IF THE SYNTAX FOR A SQL HINT IS WRONG, WHAT DOES ORACLE DO?

Oracle will simply *ignore* the hint. It is treated as a comment, with no impact on the execution plan.

IF YOU USE AN ALIAS FOR A TABLE, HOW MUST YOU SPECIFY A SQL HINT ON THAT TABLE?

You must always use the *alias* in the sql hint. This is *not* optional.

For example,

```
Select /*+FULL(ONE)*/
* from Table1 ONE
where City = 'Washington';
```

HOW CAN YOU FIX THE OPTIMIZER PROBLEM WITH "BITMAP CONVERSION FROM ROWIDS"

In recent Oracle versions, the optimizer sometimes makes a terrible mistake, opting for a tricky move called "bitmap conversion from rowids." This often results in terrible performance—sometimes 100x worse than otherwise! (The optimizer appears to badly misjudge the cost of using a non-selective index.)

You can turn off this feature at the database level (in the init.ora file), or alter any session that encounters the problem, like this:

```
Alter Session Set "_b_tree_bitmap_plans" = False;
```

When the optimizer selects the execution path, the typical execution plan will look like this:

```
SELECT STATEMENT
  SORT GROUP BY
    TABLE ACCESS BY INDEX ROWID
USER_LIST_TABLE
    NESTED LOOPS
      TABLE ACCESS FULL              USERS
      BITMAP CONVERSION TO ROWIDS
       BITMAP AND
        BITMAP CONVERSION FROM ROWIDS
          INDEX RANGE SCAN           TAB1_PK
        BITMAP CONVERSION FROM ROWIDS
          INDEX RANGE SCAN           TAB2_FK
```

IN SQL*PLUS, HOW DO YOU CHANGE THE NUMBER OF ROWS SENT TO THE CLIENT EACH TRIP?

The sql*plus parameter is called *arraysize*. It specifies how many rows to return to the client each time. This greatly impacts how many network roundtrips will be required when retrieving data. By reducing the number of network trips, overall runtime can be substantially reduced.

When transferring large amounts of data, the default setting (15) is likely not optimum. You can experiment with larger values (up to 5000) and watch the sql*net roundtrips decline. Using sql*plus *autotrace* is an easy way to do this.

Keep in mind that performance improvement will fall off drastically once the arraysize has been increased. Again, trial and error with your particular data set is a good idea.

Here's how you change the setting:

```
SQL> arraysize 1000
```

Here is how you check the current setting:

```
SQL> show arraysize
arraysize 15
```

IN THE EXECUTION PLAN FOR A PARTITIONED TABLE SCAN, WHAT DOES "KEY" MEAN?

This is a very common situation when working with execution plans related to partitioned tables (and indexes). The word "key" simply means that the optimizer *may* perform partition pruning, but that the optimizer cannot conclusively determine which partitions will be needed ahead of time.

For example, perhaps bind variables are being used, which influence which partitions are needed to resolve a query.

The exact partitions ultimately scanned will be determined at runtime. Below is an example of the optimizer using the "key" words when scanning a partitioned index:

OPERATION	OBJECT	PSTART	PSTOP
TABLE ACCESS BY LOCAL INDEX ROWID	TABLEX	KEY	KEY

The starting partition is called *Pstart*, whilst the ending partition is called *Pstop*.

IN SQL*PLUS, HOW CAN YOU STOP THE OUTPUT, AND JUST SHOW THE STATISTICIS AND EXECUTION PLAN?

This is done using *Autotrace*, like this:

```
Set Autotrace Traceonly

Select count(*) from Retail_Member;
```

```
Execution Plan
---------------------------------------------------
   0     SELECT STATEMENT Optimizer=CHOOSE (Cost=1395)
   1     0 SORT (AGGREGATE)
   2     1   INDEX (FAST FULL SCAN) OF 'RET_PK' (UNIQUE)
(Cost=1395)



Statistics
---------------------------------------------
          1   recursive calls
          2   db block gets
      23134   consistent gets
      17750   physical reads
       8336   redo size
        212   bytes sent via SQL*Net to client
        277   bytes received via SQL*Net from client
          2   SQL*Net roundtrips to/from client
          0   sorts (memory)
          0   sorts (disk)
          1   rows processed
```

WHY WOULD YOU USE A "STORED OUTLINE?"

Stored outlines are an easy way to preserve a desired execution plan. This may be done for testing purposes, or to create plan stability in production environments. Oracle accomplishes the desired plan by storing a set of sql hints, which are then applied when it recognizes the sql.

For instance, suppose you are testing a particular sql statement that is causing performance difficulties. In order to perform testing, you wish to have the execution plan on your test database match the plan that is actually run on production. To accomplish this, you capture the specific sql on the database that has the desired plan. Then, you export a few outline tables. Finally, you import these tables into the target database.

Now, whenever Oracle sees the sql, it will automatically apply the sql hints that guide the optimizer to the original execution plan.

WHAT'S THE SQL HINT FOR SPECIFYING THE *LEADING* TABLE OF A JOIN?

The hint is simply, *Leading*.

For example,

```
Select /*+LEADING(T1) */
* from Table1 T1, Table2 T2
where T1.Id = T2.Id
and T1.Name like 'Smith%'
and T2.Dept like '%Engr';
```

It is also possible to change the join order using the *Ordered* hint, but that hint is a tad more complicated than just specifying the leading table.

WHAT'S THE WAIT EVENT "LOG FILE SYNC?"

This is the delay due to writing the redo log buffers to disk.

The next question elaborates on this concept.

WHY WOULD YOU SEE EXCESSIVE WAITS FOR *LOG FILE SYNC?*

A lot of time spent waiting on log sync may be indicative of a design flaw—that is, excessive commits, but it may also indicate slow disks.

In some cases, a high commit frequency simply reflects the true business requirements of the application. There is nothing inherently wrong with frequent commits—as long as they reflect the true business requirement.

For systems with excessive commits, this wait event will be listed in the statspack or AWR report. Use this information to see how often you perform log file sync, as well as the *latency*. Here is an example, which happens to include log file sync as the #5 top wait event.

```
Top 5 Timed Events
                                                       % Total
Event                         Waits     Time (s)  Ela Time
------------------------- ------------- ----------- --------
db file sequential read     3,610,988     13,969     68.52
CPU time                                   4,553     22.33
ARCH wait on SENDREQ              789        733      3.60
db file parallel write        28,031        270      1.32
log file sync                 50,837        213      1.04
```

For the period measured by the above statspack report, the system performed 50,837 syncs, and the potential rate (i.e., for a single thread) is about $50837/213 = 238$ writes/sec. Alternatively, here is a way to estimate the rate on your system:

```
Select Event, Total_Waits,  Time_Waited ,
Round(100*Total_Waits/Time_Waited) Rate
From V$System_Event
Where Event Like '%log file sync%';

EVENT           TOTAL_WAITS TIME_WAITED       RATE
--------------- ----------- ----------- ----------
log file sync      28308678    28339804        100
```

For the system having the statistics shown above, a single session could perform about 100 log syncs per second.

HOW DO HISTOGRAMS HELP THE OPTIMIZER MAKE BETTER DECISIONS?

The purpose of histograms is to deal more accurately with *lumpy* data. If the optimizer knows how the data for a particular column is distributed, it can make a more accurate decision as to how to retrieve the data the fastest.

Oracle's histograms use a series of buckets to count the data. You might think at first that Oracle counts how many entries are in each bucket, but that's not really how it works. Instead, the width of each bucket is adjusted so that the *height* of each bucket is about the same. This method makes it easier for the optimizer.

For instance, if a column has many entries in the range 100-200, but very few in the range 1000-2000, than you might have one bucket that spans from 101 to 102, and another that spans all the way from 1000 to 2000. Although the "width" of each bucket is drastically different, the number of entries in each are about the same, due to the crazy data distribution.

You can show the histograms for a particular table by querying *Dba_histograms*. The bucket start and end values are called *endpoints*.

IN STATSPACK (OR AWR) REPORTS, WHAT SECTION SUMMARIZES WHERE MOST OF THE DATABASE TIME IS SPENT?

This section is called the "Top 5 Timed Events." Here, Oracle identifies where the time is going. Another section lists *all* the events.

Here's an example:

```
Top 5 Timed Events
~~~~~~~~~~~~~~~~~~~                                      % Total
Event                           Waits    Time (s) Ela Time
------------------------------- ------------- ----------- --------
db file sequential read         3,610,988     13,969    68.52
CPU time                                       4,553    22.33
ARCH wait on SENDREQ                  789        733     3.60
db file parallel write             28,031        270     1.32
log file sync                      50,837        213     1.04
                                ------------------------------------
```

WHAT DOES *SKIP-SCAN* MEAN?

This refers to an optimizer feature, whereby a composite index is used to resolve a query even if the column of interest is not the leading column of the index. Oracle is able to *skip* to the desired column in the index.

To accomplish skip scan, Oracle performs a separate scan for each distinct value in the prefixed index column. That is, Oracle resolves the query as if the sql had a series of values in the *where* clause—each of which calls for an index scan. Given the nature of how it works, skip scan may be a good choice, but will not be the right choice for many situations. In many cases, it will not be the best choice.

In the execution plan, a skip scan step will be noted as

```
INDEX SKIP SCAN
```

Of course, having the appropriate index, with the matching columns in the prefix, is generally best, but there may be reasons that a new index is not feasible, or perhaps the performance from skip scan proves to be good enough.

WHAT DOES *QUERY REWRITE* DO IN CONJUNCTION WITH A MATERIALIZED VIEW?

Oracle has the capability to use a materialized view to satisfy certain queries, *even if the query does not explicitly reference the view*. This feature can drastically improve response times when materialized views are able to satisfy queries that would otherwise run badly. Oracle uses the term *query rewrite* because the optimizer rewrites the sql internally so as to reference the view, and benefit from a faster execution path.

Typical uses of query rewrite are in data warehouses, where a pre-run materialized view aggregates data that is often queried by reports. For instance, you may have a view that contains cumulative sales information for each department for the entire year. Now, if a session queries the *Sales* table, asking for cumulative sales information for a certain department, the optimizer will realize that the view already has the answer, and thus switch to the materialized view.

The key restriction in using query rewrite is that the materialized view must positively contain the data needed by the candidate query. It is also necessary to have the init.ora parameter, *Query_Rewrite_Enabled* set to TRUE in order to use this functionality.

8186209R0

Made in the USA
Lexington, KY
13 January 2011